FISHING FROLICS

FISHING FROLICS

EDITED BY

P.J.M.

MICHAEL JOSEPH
LONDON

To
L.J. Young

First published in Great Britain by
Michael Joseph Limited
27 Wrights Lane, Kensington W8
1986

British Library Cataloguing in Publication Data

Fishing frolics.
1. Fishing — Anecdotes, facetiae, satire, etc.
I. P.J.M.
799.1′2′0207 SH439

ISBN 0-7181-2777-3

Typesetting by Alacrity Phototypesetters,
Banwell Castle, Weston-super-Mare
Printed and bound in Italy

An Angler's Invitation	7
A Bite At Henderson's	8
The Bait	11
The Fly Fisher	12
Spring and Summer	14
Fishing	15
Fresh Run	16
Chalk Stream Studies	18
Heredity	20
Fish, Fishing & Fishermen	23
The Secrets of Angling	24
Daydream	26
A Morning Thought	28
The Angler's Song	29
The Duffer	30
Upon A Lady's Fishing	32
Tom Brown's Schooldays	35
Fishermen's Patience	36
The Taking of the Salmon	38
Spring Salmon	41
Wading	42
To Cultivate Luck	43
The Fishermen	44
Homeward	46
Acknowledgements	48

THE ANGLER'S INVITATION

Come when the leaf comes, angle with me,
  Come when the bee hums over the lea,
    Come with the wild flowers,
    Come with the mild showers,
Come when the singing bird calleth for thee!

Then to the stream side, gladly we'll hie,
Where the grey trout glide silently by,
    Or in some still place
    Over the hill face
Hurrying onward, drop the light fly.

Then, when the dew falls, homeward we'll speed
To our own loved walls down on the mead,
    There, by the bright hearth,
    Holding our night mirth,
We'll drink to sweet friendship in need and in deed.

THOMAS TOD STODDART

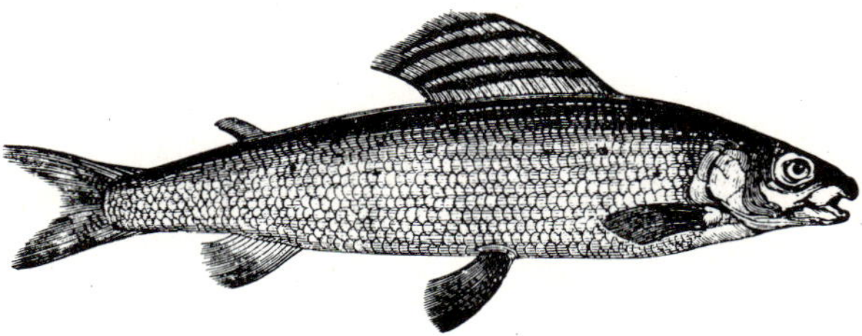

A BITE AT HENDERSON'S

MY FIRST TROUT. — Oh, joy of joys! As I approached my tenth year I became more and more devoted to my fishing-rod, and with a little knot of friends as enthusiastic as myself, I used to pass every hour unclaimed by our schoolmaster in spinning hair-lines, making tackle and bobbing for eels.

On one of our holiday afternoons the little party of friends repaired to the Browney, near Langley Bridge, and there in the long Dub by the side of the Brancepeth road we propped our rods side by side and began a game at leap-frog, when a cry arose, "There's a bite at Henderson's." A rush to the river, an anxious pause, a gentle uplifting of the rod, a loud scream of wonder and backwards I ran, far into the dusty road, dragging a trout whose weight was at least a pound. The war-whoops and dances of a party of Indians could hardly have exceeded the excitement to which we gave way. There was cheer upon cheer, yell upon yell, and many a thump descended upon my back in token of sympathy. There was no more fishing that afternoon. Back we marched to the old city, bearing our prize suspended by the gills upon a hazel stick and looking out for the admiring gaze of the passers-by. The Iron Duke, when Waterloo had been fought and won, was not more proud than we.

WILLIAM HENDERSON

1863
DALZIEL

from

THE BAIT

Come live with me, and be my love,
And we will some new pleasures prove,
Of golden sands and crystal brooks,
With silken lines and silver hooks.

There will the river whisp'ring run,
Warm'd by thy eyes more than the sun;
And there th' inamor'd fish will stay,
Begging themselves they may betray.

When thou wilt swim in that live bath,
Each fish, which every channel hath,
Will amorously to thee swim,
Gladder to catch thee, than thou him.

Let others freeze with angling reeds,
And cut their legs with shells and weeds,
Or treacherously poor fish beset,
With strangling snare or windowy net:

Let coarse bold hands, from slimy nest,
The bedded fish in banks outwrest;
Or curious traitors, sleave-silk flies,
Bewitch poor fishes' wandering eyes.

For thee, thou need'st no such deceit,
For thou thyself art thine own bait;
That fish that is not catch'd thereby
Alas! is wiser far than I.

JOHN DONNE

THE FLY-FISHER

Just in the dubious point where with the pool
Is mixed the trembling stream, or where it boils
Around the stone, or from the hollowed bank
Reverted plays in undulating flow,
There throw, nice-judging, the delusive fly;
And, as you lead it round in artful curve,
With eye attentive mark the springing game.
Straight as above the surface of the flood
They wanton rise, or urged by hunger leap,
Then fix with gentle twitch the barbed hook —
Some lightly tossing to the grassy bank,
And to the shelving shore slow-dragging some,
With various hand proportioned to their force.
If, yet too young and easily deceived,
A worthless prey scarce bends your pliant rod,
Him, piteous of his youth and the short space
He has enjoyed the vital light of heaven,
Soft disengage, and back into the stream
The speckled infant throw. But, should you lure
From his dark haunt beneath the tangled roots
Of pendent trees the monarch of the brook,
Behoves you then to ply your finest art.
Long time he, following cautious, scans the fly,
And oft attempts to seize it, but as oft
The dimpled water speaks his jealous fear.
At last, while haply o'er the shaded sun
Passes a cloud, he desperate takes the death
With sullen plunge. At once he darts along,
Deep-struck, and runs out all the lengthened line;

Then seeks the farthest ooze, the sheltering weed,
The caverned bank, his old secure abode;
And flies aloft, and flounces round the pool,
Indignant of the guile. With yielding hand,
That feels him still, yet to his furious course
Gives way, you, now retiring, following now
Across the stream, exhaust his idle rage;
Till floating broad upon his breathless side,
And to his fate abandoned, to the shore
You gaily drag your unresisting prize.

JAMES THOMSON

SPRING AND SUMMER

COMES APRIL, and desire is off to the valleys between the mountains, where streams are boisterous and little trout leap in the foam; where the wind comes sparkling off the moors, and a man feels a new life stirring within him. But in July, when the world croons the summer song of heat and light and slumbrous days, it is to the deep, slow river with its cool wealth of shade, and the solemn music of the weir, that we wander for refreshment, there to watch a daintily poised float, or to cozen old loggerhead out of his fastness of lily-pads with an artificial bumblebee.

H. T. SHERINGHAM

FISHING

Fishing, if I, a fisher, may protest,
Of pleasures is the sweetest, of sports the best,
Of exercises the most excellent;
Of recreations the most innocent;
But now the sport is marde, and wott ye why?
Fishes decrease, and fishers multiply.

THOMAS BASTARD

FRESH RUN

Well hooked, but far from beaten yet,
He plays a gallant fighting part.
My nerves are strung, my teeth are set,
My brow, and more of me, is wet
With what is surely honest sweat —
Who christened this the "gentle art?"

Just where the swirling rapids flash,
He took me with a sudden dart,
Then came a pull, a sounding splash,
A whirring reel, a furious dash,
Then over boulders, leap and crash —
Who christened this the "gentle art?"

So lumbering onwards blown and spent,
These forty minutes from the start
I have pursued where'er he went,
The rovings of his discontent,
My greenheart to a crescent bent —
Who christened this the "gentle art?"

Spectators watch with eager eyes,
They shout together and apart:
"Be gentle with him," some advise;
"Give him the butt," another cries;
Their clamour mounts unto the skies —
Who christened this the "gentle art?"

He girds him for his final play,
And I, with victory at my heart,
Summon the gaff to end him. Nay!
My line sags emptily away —
Shade of old Izaak, what to say?
Who christened this the "gentle art?"

ALFRED COCHRANE

A MERRY CHRISTMAS.

from

CHALK STREAM STUDIES

COME, THEN, you who want pleasant fishing days without the waste of time and trouble and expense involved in two hundred miles of railway journey, and perhaps fifty more of highland road, and try what you can see and do among the fish not fifty miles from town. Come to pleasant country inns, where you can always get a good dinner; or, better still, to pleasant country houses, where you can always get good society; to rivers which will always fish, brimfull in the longest droughts of summer, instead of being, as those mountain ones are, very like a turnpike-road for three weeks, and then like bottled porter for three days; to streams on which you have strong south-west breezes for a week together on a clear fishing water, instead of having, as on those mountain ones, foul rain 'spate' as long as the wind is south-west, and clearing water when the wind chops up to the north, and the chill blast of 'Clarus Aquilo' sends all the fish shivering to the bottom; streams, in a word, where you may kill fish (and large ones) four days out of five from April to October, instead of having, as you will most probably in the mountain, just one day's sport in the whole of your month's holiday. Deluded friend, who suffered in Scotland last year a month of Tantalus his torments, furnished by art and nature with rods, flies, whisky, scenery, keepers, salmon innumerable, and all that man can want, except water to fish in; and who returned, having hooked accidentally by the tail one salmon — which broke all and went to sea — why did you not stay at home and take your two-pounders and three-pounders out of the quiet chalk brook which never sank an inch through all that drought, so deep in the caverns of the hills are hidden its mysterious wells?

Repent, then; and come with me, at least in fancy, at six o'clock upon some breezy morning in the end of June, not by roaring railway nor by smoking steamer, but in the cosy four-wheel, along brown heather moors, down into green clay woodlands, over white chalk downs, past Roman camps and scattered blocks of Sarsden stone, till we descend into the long green vale where, among groves of poplar and abele, winds silver Whit. Come and breakfast at the neat white inn, of yore a posting-house of fame which keeps up enough of its ancient virtue to give us a breakfast worthy of Pantagruel's self.

CHARLES KINGSLEY

from

HEREDITY

Treat children's sport with laughter,
  Or, if you will, with tears;
Such joy comes not hereafter,
  Through all our later years.
We scarcely now can measure
  By backward cast of thought,
The ecstasy of pleasure
  Crushed from the lees of sport.

Though years may rend in sunder—
  And what will time not rend?—
The bright thin line of wonder,
  With mystery at the end:
Yet passion's quenchless ember
  Is with us even yet:
Through children we remember
  What else we might forget.

We watch the eager glances
  By keen expectance cast,
To where the light float dances
  In every playful blast.
Below, what hidden treasure
  May now be hovering near,
Pausing, to add to pleasure
  A spice of groundless fear.

The net is waiting ready
  Its prize to safely fold,
Keep eye and hand both steady,
  Nor slacken now your hold.
Grant but a scanty measure
  Of line, lest he regain
His earlier flower of pleasure,
  Your latter leaf of pain.

'Tis done. Among the rushes
His glittering body lies,
Excitement throbs in blushes,
Light dances in the eyes.
I feel the dying ember
Of sport burns in me yet.
What childhood's days remember
Age scarcely will forget.

ANON.

from

FISH, FISHING AND FISHERMEN

It is a lie that fishermen lie.

A lie is a statement made with intent to deceive. No fisherman makes such statements. For since every fisherman to whom another fisherman asserts that, on such a day and in such a place, he slew so many trouts or barbels or whitebaits, weighing so much — since every such first fisherman automatically divides number and weight by three, halves that and knocks off ninety per cent from the quotient (or whatever it is), he — I mean the first fisherman — when in his turn he tells a story of the same sort to yet another, a third fisherman, confidently expects that third fisherman to treat his (the first's) in the same fashion. Now such a man may not justly be accused of lying. He does no more than follow a well-recognized and convenient custom.

When I tell you — supposing you to be what some people call A Brother of the Angle — that in one day I killed two hundred trouts weighing exactly two hundred pounds the last time I fished the Barle at Dulverton, you will not for a moment imagine that I am trying to deceive you, but will simply understand that I am speaking of a rather unusually good bit of sport I have once had, and that I did, perhaps, in actual fact, kill sixteen trouts weighing all together fifty ounces.

This instinctive and generous (or is it jealous?) discount which fishermen allow to one another's statements alone perfectly explains why those statements are so generously conceived. It is cruel and wicked and quite unnecessary to assume that they are prompted by any sort of wish to deceive. If I tell another disciple (as they say) of Walton that I have caught — and I speak the very truth — sixteen trouts weighing fifty ounces in the Barle at Dulverton, which mark you, is a very fine performance, he will take me to have meant that I have caught one fish weighing one ounce and risen two others of unknown size. And instead of his admiration, which is my due, I shall earn his contempt, which would be unfair. In order, therefore, to make him understand precisely what happened, I am compelled to speak in hundreds of fishes and in hundreds of pounds.

Fishermen are simply confirmed and painstaking truthtellers, who all happen to react a little feebly to a certain kind of stimulus.

No; if it's liars you're looking for don't search the banks of a stream. Go to the golf-links.

William Caine

from

THE SECRETS OF ANGLING

Let me live harmlessly, and near the brink
Of Trent or Avon have a dwelling place,
Where I may see my quil or cork down sink,
With eager bit of Pearch, or Bleak, or Dace;
And on the world and my Creator think,
Whilst some men strive, ill gotten goods t'imbrace;
  And others spend their time in base excess
  Of wine or worse, in war and wantonness.

The loftie woods, the Forrests wide and long
Adorn'd with leaves and branches fresh and green,
In whose cool bowres the birds with many a song
Do welcom with their Quire the Summers Queen:
The Meadows fair, where Flora's gifts among
Are intermixt, with verdant grass between.
  The silver-scaled fish that softly swim,
  Within the sweet brooks chrystal watry stream.

All these, and many more of his Creation,
That made the Heavens, the Angler oft doth see,
Taking therein no little delectation,
To think how strange, how wonderful they be;
Framing thereof an inward contemplation,
To set his heart from other fancies free;
  And whilst he looks on them with joyful eye
  His mind is rapt above the Starry Skie.

JOHN DENNYS (edited by Isaak Walton)

DAYDREAM

(Written before the destruction by enemy action
of the Chamber of the Commons)

Methought my prison-house did fall away
And vanish wholly in our London air,
The Table, too, and Mr Speaker's chair,
The Mace, the Serjeant, and the flushed array
of worthy wearied senators a-doze
On the green benches.
And I saw at play
The trout of Boxford Mill and the wild rose
Open its fragrance to the summer day.
Pale iris flames I saw adown the stream,
Frothed meadowsweet and loosestrife pointing
nigh
Clusters of purple spires, and in my dream
I heard the snipe bleat in the golden sky.

* * * * *

"Awake!" one said, "They're asking what's ado
In the vexed realms from China to Peru."

LORD HARMSWORTH

A MORNING THOUGHT

No more, no more will I
    resign
  My couch so warm and soft,
To trouble trout with hook and
    line
  That will not spring aloft.

With larks appointments one
    may fix
  To greet the dawning skies,
But hang the getting up
    at six,
  For fish that will not *rise!*

THOMAS HOOD

THE ANGLERS SONG

As inward love breeds outward talk,
The Hound some praise, and some the Hawk,
Some better pleas'd with private sport,
Use Tenis, some a Mistris court:
  But these delights I neither wish,
  Nor envy, while I freely fish.

Who hunts, doth oft in danger ride;
Who hauks, lures oft both far and wide;
Who uses games, may often prove
A loser; but who fals in love,
  Is fettered in fond Cupids snare:
  My Angle breeds me no such care.

Of Recreation there is none
So free as fishing is alone;
All other pastimes do no less
Than mind and body both possess;
  My hand alone my work can do,
  So I can fish and study too.

The first men that our Saviour dear
Did chuse to wait upon him here,
Blest Fishers were; and fish the last
Food was, that he on earth did taste:
  I therefore strive to follow those,
  Whom he to follow him hath chose.

WILLIAM BASSE

THE DUFFER

I CAN'T KEEP a fly-book. I stuff the flies into my pockets at random, or stick them into the leaves of a novel, or bestow them in the lining of my hat or the case of my rods. Never in all my days did I possess a landing-net. If I can drag a fish up a bank, or over the gravel, well; if not, he goes on his way rejoicing. A landing-net is a tedious thing to carry, so is a creel, and a creel is, to me, a superfluity. There is never anything to put

in it. If I do catch a trout, I lay him under a big stone, cover him with leaves, and never find him again. I often break my top joint; so, as I never carry string, I splice it with a bit of the line, which I bite off, for I really cannot be troubled with scissors and I always lose my knife. When a phantom minnow sticks in my clothes, I snap the gut off, and put on another, so that when I reach home I look as if a shoal of fierce minnows had attacked me and hung on like leeches. When a boy, I was — once or twice — a bait-fisher, but I never carried worms in box or bag. I found them under big stones, or in the fields, whenever I had the luck. I never tie nor otherwise fasten the joints of my rod; they often slip out of the sockets and splash into the water. Mr. Hardy, however, has invented a joint-fastening which never slips. On the other hand, by letting the joint rust, you may find it difficult to take down your rod. When I see a trout rising, I always cast so as to get hung up, and I frighten him as I disengage my hook. I invariably fall in and get half drowned when I wade, there being an insufficiency of nails in the soles of my brogues. My waders let in water, too, and when I go out to fish I usually leave either my reel, or my flies, or my rod, at home.

ANDREW LANG

UPON A LADY'S FISHING WITH AN ANGLE.

See where the fair Clorinda sits, and seems
Like new-born Venus risen from the streams;
In vain the beauties of the neighbouring field,
In vain the painted flowers' pride
With their faint colours strive to hide
That flower to which Flora herself would yield.
Each object's pleasant to the sight,
The streams, the meadows yield delight,
But nothing fair as her you can espy
Unless i' th' brook (her looking-glass) you chance to cast your eye.

See how she makes the trembling angle shake,
Touched by those hands that would make all men quake.
See how the numerous fishes of the brook
    (For now the armour of their scales
    Nothing against her charms prevails)
Willingly hang themselves upon her hook;
    See how they crowd and thronging wait
    Greedy to catch the proffered bait;
In her more bright and smoother hands content
Rather to die, than live in their own watery element.

With how composed a look and cheerful air,
(Calm as the stream and as the season fair)
With careful eyes she views the dancing float,
    Longing to have it disappear,
    That she its head may higher rear,
And make it swim i' th' air above the moat;
    She sits as silent as the fish,
    Seems burdened with no other wish,
So well she's masked under this fair pretence,
An infidel would swear she's made of perfect innocence.

But ah! Clorinda's is a cruel game,
As she with water sports, she sports with flame,
She innocently angles here, but then
    Thousands of charming baits she lays,
    A thousand other several ways;
Her beauteous eyes ensnare whole shoals of men,
    Each golden hair's a fishing line,
    Able to catch such hearts as mine,
And he that once views her bewitching eyes,
To her victorious charms (like me) must ever be a prize.

EDMUND WALLER

R F M
Christmas Greetings
Aggravation
COPYRIGHT

from

TOM BROWN'S SCHOOLDAYS

Now came on the may-fly season; the soft hazy summer weather lay sleepily along the rich meadows by Avon-side, and the green and grey flies flickered with their graceful lazy up-and-down flight over the reeds and the water and the meadows in myriads upon myriads. The may-flies must surely be the lotus-eaters of the ephemerae: the happiest, laziest, carelessest fly that dances and dreams out his few hours of sunshiny life by English rivers.

So, one fine Thursday afternoon, Tom, having borrowed East's new rod, started by himself to the river. He fished for some time with small success, not a fish would rise at him; but, as he prowled along the bank, he was presently aware of mighty ones feeding in a pool on the opposite side, under the shade of a huge willow tree. The stream was deep here, but some fifty yards below was a shallow, for which he made off hot-foot; and forgetting landlords, keepers, solemn prohibitions of the doctor, and everything else, pulled up his trousers, plunged across, and in three minutes was creeping along on all fours towards the clump of willows.

It isn't often that great chub, or any other coarse fish, are in earnest about anything, but just then they were thoroughly bent on feeding, and in half-an-hour Master Tom had deposited three thumping fellows at the foot of the giant willow.

THOMAS HUGHES

from

ROD AND LINE

NOTHING IS MORE trying to the patience of fishermen than the remark so often made to them by the profane: 'I have not patience enough for fishing'. It is not so much the remark itself (showing a complete and forgivable ignorance of angling as it does) that is annoying as the manner in which it is said, the kindly condescending manner in which Ulysses might tell Penelope that he had not patience for needlework. What are they, these dashing, impatient sparks? Are they d'Artagnans all, rough-riders, playboys of a western world, wild desperate fellows who look for a spice of danger in their pleasure? Not a bit of it. They hit a ball backwards and forwards over a net or submit to the patient drudgery of golf, a laborious form of open-air patience in which you hit a ball, walk earnestly after it and hit it again. These devotees of monotonous artificial pleasures who say that fishing is too slow a game for them seem to imagine that fishing is a sedentary occupation. Let them put on waders and fish up a full river and then walk down it on a hot summer day. Let them combine for an afternoon the arts of the Red Indian and the mountaineer and, in the intervals of crawling through brambles and clambering over boulders, keep cool enough to fill a basket with the up-stream worm. Let them discover that they have to take their coats off when salmon fishing on a day when the line freezes in the rings. Let them spin for pike in February, or trout in August. They will find that they get exercise enough. Some forms of fishing are sedentary, in the purely physical sense, in that after a man has baited a spot for carp or roach, or anchored a boat for perch, he keeps still. But he has not attained a sort of Nirvana, like a crystal gazer, isolating himself from nature by concentration on a miserable ball. His mind is not dulled but lively with expectation and, of all the virtues, patience is the one he least requires. Of all kinds of fishing only one requires patience and that is trailing a bait after a boat when someone else is doing the rowing. Even in those forms of fishing which do not mean moving about, it never occurs to an angler to pride himself on his patience. Self-control, if you like, but not the most leisurely of all the virtues. There would be patience needed to watch a float which (there being no fish in the water) you knew would never budge, but none in watching a float that may at any moment make a demand for instant action.

ARTHUR RANSOME

THE TAKING OF THE SALMON

A birr! a whirr! a salmon's on,
  A goodly fish! a thumper!
Bring up, bring up the ready gaff,
And if we land him, we shall quaff
  Another glorious bumper!
  Hark! 'tis the music of the reel,
    The strong, the quick, the steady;
  The line darts from the active wheel —
    Have all things right and ready.

A birr! a whirr! the salmon's out,
Far on the rushing river;
Onward he holds with sudden leap,
Or plunges through the whirlpool deep,
A desperate endeavour!
Hark to the music of the reel!
The fitful and the grating:
It pants along the breathless wheel,
Now hurried — now abating.

A birr! a whirr! the salmon's off! —
No, no, we still have got him;
The wily fish is sullen grown,
And, like a bright imbedded stone,
Lies gleaming at the bottom.
Hark to the music of the reel!
'Tis hush'd, it hath forsaken;
With care we'll guard the magic wheel,
Until its notes rewaken.

A birr! a whirr! the salmon's up,
Give line, give line and measure:
But now he turns! keep down ahead,
And lead him as a child is led,
And land him at your leisure.
Hark to the music of the reel!
'Tis welcome, it is glorious;
It wanders through the winding wheel,
Returning and victorious.

A birr! a whirr! the salmon's in,
   Upon the bank extended;
The princely fish is gasping slow,
His brilliant colours come and go,
   All beautifully blended.
   Hark to the music of the reel,
      It murmurs and it closes:
   Silence is on the conquering wheel,
      Its wearied line reposes.

No birr! no whirr! the salmon's ours,
   The noble fish, the thumper:
Strike through his gill the ready gaff,
And bending homewards, we shall quaff
   Another glorious bumper!
   Hark to the music of the reel,
      We listen with devotion;
   There's something in that circling wheel
      That wakes the heart's emotion!

THOMAS TOD STODDART

SPRING SALMON

It's oh, but I'm dreaming
Of grey water streaming,
Great rivers that go gleaming
   Where brown the heather blows,
Ere May's southern graces
Rub out the last white traces
From high and mountain places
   Of stubborn, storm-packed snows!

The chill wind that searches
The low-lying birches,
The old red grouse that perches
   And swaggers in the sun;
I'm fain for its blowing,
I'm restless for his crowing,
And it's I that would be going
   Where the spring salmon run!

PATRICK CHALMERS

WILLIAM SCROPE'S WAY OF WADING

WADING IN the water is not only an agreeable thing in itself, but absolutely necessary in some rivers in the North that are destitute of boats; and that you may do this in the best possible style, procure half a dozen pair of shoes, with large knob-nails at some distance asunder; if they are too close, they will bring your foot to an even surface, and it will glide off a stone or rock, which in deep water may be inconvenient. Cut some holes in the upper-leathers of your shoes, to give the water a free passage out of them when you are on dry land; not because the fluid is annoying, for we should wrong you to say so, but to prevent the pumping noise you would otherwise make at every step. If you are not much of a triton, you may use fishermen's boots, and keep yourself dry: it is all a matter of taste. When you are wading through the rapids, step on quickly and boldly, and do not gaze down on the stream after the fashion of Narcissus: for running waves will not reflect your beauty, but only make your head giddy. If you stop for a moment, place your legs abreast of each other: should you fancy a straddle, with one of them in advance, the action of the water will operate upon both, trip you up, and carry you out to sea.

Avoid standing upon rocking stones, for obvious reasons; and never go into the water deeper than the fifth button of your waistcoat; even this does not always agree with tender constitutions in frosty weather. As you are likely not to take a just estimate of the cold in the excitement of the sport, should you be of a delicate temperament, and be wading in the month of February, when it may chance to freeze very hard, pull down your stockings, and examine your legs. Should they be black, or even purple, it might, perhaps, be as well to get on dry land; but if they are only rubicund, you may continue to enjoy the water, if it so pleases you.

WILLIAM SCROPE

from

TO CULTIVATE LUCK

IT IS CERTAIN that good luck is the most vital part of the equipment of him who would seek to slay big carp. For some men I admit the usefulness of skill and pertinacity; for myself, I take my stand entirely on luck. To the novice I would say: Cultivate your luck. Prop it up with omens and signs of good purport. Watch for magpies on your path. Form the habit of avoiding old women who squint. Throw salt over your left shoulder. Touch wood with the forefinger of your right hand whenever you are not doing anything else. Be on friendly terms with a black cat. Turn your money under the new moon. Walk round ladders. Don't start on a Friday. Stir the materials for Christmas pudding and wish. Perform all other such rites as you know or hear of. These things are important in carp-fishing.

H. T. SHERINGHAM

from

THE FISHERMEN

The quiet pastime of their choice
  On Beauly rocks, in Derwent glades,
Still seems to move to Walton's voice,
  Singing of dace and dairymaids:
His water meadows still are wet,
  His brawling trout-streams leap and glance,
And on their sunlit ripples yet
  The flies of his disciples dance.

Anglers complete and incomplete,
  The expert or the 'prentice hand,
In friendly rivalry they meet
  By loch and river, sedge and sand;
Enthusiasts all, of staid address,
  They go their way from cast to cast,
Alike in failure or success,
  Sanguine and serious to the last.

Then, when their pensive task is done,
  The wayside hostel's chimney seat
Finds them, good comrades every one,
  Prepared their exploits to repeat;
Each has his shifts of sight and touch,
  His own expedients each admires,
Each follows still, though not too much,
  His own devices and desires.

ALFRED COCHRANE

HOMEWARD

When homeward from the stream we turn
  Good cheer our sport replaces,
There's liquor twinkling in the glass,
  There's joy on all our faces!

We drink sweet healths, a merry round,
  We talk old stories over,
And sing glad staves, like summer birds
  Below their leafy cover.

Thus cheerily our evenings pass,
  Till lulled below the quilting
We sleep our toils off, and are forth
  Before the lark is lilting.

All joy be with our hearts' kin bold!
  May care's nets ne'er entangle,
Nor woe nor poverty depress
  A brother of the angle!

THOMAS TOD STODDART

ACKNOWLEDGEMENTS

The editor and publishers wish to thank the following publishers for permission to quote: the Longman Group Limited for the two poems from *Collected Verses* by Alfred Cochrane; Frederick Muller Limited for 'Daydream' from *A Little Fishing Book* by Cecil, Lord Harmsworth, Jonathan Cape for the extract from *Rod and Line* by Arthur Ransome and Methuen & Co Limited for the verses from 'Spring Salmon' by Patrick Chalmers from *Green Days and Blue Days*.

The illustrations on pages 6, 20, 22, 25, 27 and 47 appear by courtesy of the Bridgeman Art Library; those on pages 11, and 19 by the Mary Evans Picture Library; that on page 33 by the Radio Times Hulton Picture Library; that on page 41 by the Mansell Collection and those on pages 9, 15, 30 and 37, by the proprietors of Punch.
I have been unable to trace the owners of certain copyrights and beg the forgiveness of anyone whose rights have been overlooked.